TARGETED
Make Change Happen

TARGETED
Make Change Happen

LIZ SHERMAN

TARGETED
MAKE CHANGE HAPPEN

iUniverse books may be ordered through booksellers or by contacting:

iUniverse
1663 Liberty Drive
Bloomington, IN 47403
www.iuniverse.com
1-800-Authors (1-800-288-4677)

ISBN: 978-1-5320-3579-1 (sc)
ISBN: 978-1-5320-3580-7 (e)

Library of Congress Control Number: 2017916552

Print information available on the last page.

iUniverse rev. date: 11/03/2017

Introduction

Today is the kind of day that makes me feel I should get something accomplished; it's raining and dull. An indoor activity could be beneficial.

I'm just an average Canadian citizen who has been around for a while. I'd like to comment on the progress (or lack of it) in our government and how the low-income class has become the bottom rung in the ladder. It seems so from my perspective anyway. I have seen prosperity in my time, but things have been going downhill for a long time.

In this book I'll use a few personal examples, as well as examples of what others have faced in their lifetimes. My questions are directed at the leaders of Canada and the province of Ontario in particular. I will make reference to others only as they are similar to our situation and perhaps how they handled their problems. I don't blame anyone in particular, but I point out where, in my opinion, some of this insecurity has occurred.

Unequivocally, Canada is the best, most beautiful country ever, with gracious citizens who harbor no ill toward others. That is a reputation we Canadians value and hold dear. On the whole, we have come a long way, but now things are getting to the point where we need help from whatever sources we can muster.

I'm not an expert on these subjects, but I what I have to say is important enough to write about it, for us and for our future generations.

History tells us how the economy was dealt with in the past and how it has evolved. So we are able to determine almost what should work and what won't. Our whole culture is changing, and there is always unrest with change. We are comfortable with our old habits and the particular culture to which we've grown accustomed. These are the things that make us feel safe and secure. Change, however, is inevitable.

As time moves forward, so do we. We have grown so much in the last fifty years and have advanced rapidly, to a point that would have been unbelievable just a short time ago.

It could be lack of communication, a huge oversight, or ignorance of our dilemma, or maybe it's a combination of all three, but a lot of us cannot cope in these modern times. We simply do not have the tools to deal with it. Perhaps we need to speak up as groups so we can cover all the bases. One thing is certain: we can't go on this way much longer. We need professional assistance in dealing with our immediate problems.

What has happened in the past does not help matters. In fact, I think it is worse now.

Chapter 1

THE GOOD OLD DAYS

I don't know why I feel that injustice has been done to us by the powers that be in our lives. It's a feeling, however, that just won't go away. Sometimes I feel strongly about it, and other times I simply feel it.

My life has been uneventful. I have four grown, independent children and have gone through both rough patches and good times. All this upheaval has brought me to *now*, and I have to question things of importance to me and to many others.

In today's society, I am one of the people who make up the average sector, simply trying to make my way financially and morally, without trouble or incident, and trying to fit in and get along, as are many others at my level, which I consider the middle working class.

I started out in a poor family with a lot of children in a small town in Ontario, where almost everyone was in the same boat, although some were a bit better off than we were. My family didn't feel poor, as everyone in our area had a level of poverty in common. We were all very similar in status, and that was the norm. Of course, life was simpler back then. Even though we didn't go hungry, food often was sparse—let's say we ate lightly at times, but we never starved. Our parents were very good to my siblings and me, and they loved us unconditionally, which made for happy, content lives, if not social prominence. I think the saying "Ignorance is bliss" must be true. We survived nicely in our little piece of the universe. The biggest part of life was spent outdoors, playing with neighbor children until the streetlights came on. Then it was time to go home for supper and bed. We had board games, and of course we played hockey and ball and other inexpensive outdoor activities. We never seemed to be at a loss for things to do. One thing is certain: we all had good imaginations.

Luckily, some of the adult residents would invite us children to an evening every week in the church basement to learn to sew and do leather crafts—and maybe darts or art. A lovely couple who just liked children had us over to their yard on the weekends to teach archery. We seemed to have different programs to keep us busy, and most of us went every week and enjoyed it. As we got older, the couple would run dances for the young teens and supervise us there as well.

It was actually a unique community, where we all were watched over by the adults, and we were cared for by the community of grown-ups if we happened to cut ourselves or fall off bikes or have other mishaps. When I think of it now, I guess it was special—sort of an early community watch—and most people donated time here and there. I realize now how secure we were as children.

It's funny how we have so much more now in almost every avenue of life, yet we think of our childhood years ago as the good old days. Go figure.

Chapter 2

WHAT IS PROSPERITY?

Is the priority really the citizens of our country or prosperity for the already well-to-do?

That is a major concern for the average low-income earners. I cannot grasp the concept of so many being seemingly left behind when it comes to reasonable prosperity. My brain cannot wrap itself around some of the things that are directed at the average middle- or lower-income population. Some things that have gone forward in my lifetime don't add up. I realize how easy it is to get caught up in our own circumstances, so much so that we tend to dwell only on our own problems. So many people, however, need a hand or a handout from those who can manage it. They are literally at the ends of their ropes, financially, mentally, and morally. The problem is crucial, and someone must do something about it—someone with the power, funds, and ability to accomplish results.

It seems as though our part of the world is trying to cater to the well-off. Current advertisements show mostly prosperous people and the upper class, the ones you can be sure will be able to take advantage of the upscale goods in the ads. That is nice for them, but what are the average- and low-income people to do? The second-hand shops are becoming the stores of choice now for a lot of people, and even they are raising prices to the point where sometimes you can get better prices at the big-box stores.

We need more things now to satisfy our personal needs and make us happy. It's not unusual to see two or even three cars in the driveway, televisions in every room, lots of extra rooms in the houses, and great yards to lounge in. They are all good but expensive and are considered necessities by many. There's been so much progress in such a short time. As we look at the expectations of young couples starting out, there is much more anxiety about obtaining worldly goods. It's almost as if it's an unwritten rule that a person has to acquire certain items to fit in with the mainstream. It does appear to be much ado about nothing, though. Stress is taken on for appearances, not by necessity. Everyone wants to start out fully equipped, but there is something about working together and achieving these goals over time that is gratifying as well.

When couples get married or have children, many register at high-end stores for gifts. Some can probably afford to shop and spend like that, but many cannot, and it makes those people feel less able.

Rather than shopping for a gift, I have taken to giving a money card with what I feel is sufficient for certain events.

Chapter 3

INDUSTRY

I started in the workforce long ago. I have worked for a few companies, some better than others, but I did enjoy most of them. I stayed employed for the better part of thirty-five years, learning and progressing along the way. That's the way it was done back then. I consider myself lucky to have been of working age when working in industry was respected and provided many jobs. I was able to look for work one day and start working the next day. I was instructed and trained in specifics of the industry at the time I was hired. In those days, a company would hire and train its employees, and the company expected those employees to stay with them, usually until retirement.

I was grateful because I ended up with wonderful qualifications that were to my benefit later on. I recognized the opportunity these companies gave me, and I worked hard for them. Ultimately it was beneficial for both the company and me. More often than not, a person could move up the ladder quite quickly if he or she was motivated and would earn a nice take-home pay to boot.

I never got wealthy, but I am provided for now and have no worries of the kind I'm writing about, as long as I stay within my personal budget. I am able to have a night out once in a while for entertainment. I only need to survive and be healthy to be happy.

My family is my happiness; I hate to see them or anyone else feel hopeless and alone, struggling to make ends meet.

If we can possibly do things that will improve the quality of life for others, let's at least try. Things don't seem as simple now, and families don't have as many choices. Everything is decidedly more difficult to achieve in this highly competitive time. There is more strife in our society. Of course there are those who didn't accomplish as much as others. Perhaps they didn't get the raises and benefits to grow with the cost-of-living index. Perhaps it was just the times that affected them. At one point companies let higher-income earners go in order to hire cheaper labor. A lot of industry left the province to reestablish the companies in countries where they could pay much cheaper wages. Whatever the reason, these people are behind the grid and cannot keep pace financially. With lower wages and a higher cost of living, it's going to be a long time before we see any real difference. I think changes need to be implemented.

Chapter 4

THE FIRST REALIZATION

I'd been working for a few years and was happy at my job. I had lovely people coworkers at a good company. They treated me well, and I enjoyed going to work each day.

The first time I noticed a difference in what I considered to be a normal, healthy employee/management relationship was a conflict that began when I hurt myself at work. Clearly, it was an accident that could have been prevented—the seat of my chair broke, and I fell to the floor in a tangled mess. My leg somehow was caught under the metal arm, and I banged my head hard on the floor.

My supervisor was sitting next to me at the same workstation, and she witnessed this. Because I was embarrassed by the fall in front of my colleagues, I got up too quickly and promptly fell down again; my head was hurting. My supervisor had someone call for an ambulance. I was told later that my chair was supposed to have been removed from the work area, as someone else had already fallen off it when it had broken previously.

I was taken to the hospital and evaluated. The doctor told me to go home and rest and to take over-the-counter pain relief, as there were no broken bones. My head injury, however, might take a while to heal.

The crux of the issue is that when the Workers' Compensation

Board (WCB) came to investigate, the chair was nowhere to be found. Ultimately, it was my word against the company's. I was not a new employee; I had been there for a few years, so I naturally thought they would believe my explanation of what had happened. That was not to be, and for the first time in my life I felt intimidated by my employer. They did not want to compensate me for my time off or for my injury.

I ultimately received what was owed to me and went back to work feeling better, but from that time on, my idea of fair play always came to mind when negotiating for promotions and increases. Never did I accept anyone's word at face value, and I learned to be wary and to protect myself.

My health started to present little problems for me. It wasn't noticeable to others, but I felt a difference in my stamina. I learned from experience that we are ultimately responsible for our own well-being. If you have to take charge, then do it, even if you feel self-conscious. I felt that things were not going in my favor, but I felt helpless and inadequate against those who I considered my superiors. Then, my sense of fair play took over for my personal rights. That new attitude served me well for the rest of my career. It made me stronger.

I imagined that the truth would speak for itself. How naive of me. I persevered, answered every query, and stood firm. I came to realize it wasn't my coworkers or immediate supervisors who argued; it was the insurance company. I never dreamed they would balk at compensating a loyal employee. I assumed they would do the right thing, but it was not that way at all. Eventually, as I mentioned, I received compensation for my efforts. That chair, however, never was seen again. That makes me suspicious.

Today, insurance companies aren't concerned with keeping their policies secret. They seem to revel in letting the public know that if you need to file an insurance claim, you'd better have a darn good one, or you likely won't receive it, at least not without a fight. I duly noted that truth, and I learned from that harrowing experience that

I needed to stand up for my rights and defend myself. It took a lot of pressure off me when I realized that was the way claims generally were handled. I didn't have any knowledge of the system when I started that process; I learned over time, through conversations with others, that rejection of new claims was normal procedure for many insurance companies.

Chapter 5

KEEPING UP

I resumed my career as an administrator, although I changed jobs. My former company was downsizing, and I took the "golden handshake" before they had layoffs. It was obvious that the workload was diminishing, and it was only a matter of time before the company went out of business. So I returned to school, taking a couple of courses at night. That was the start of my next adventure.

I was working and enjoying my position and the new friends I had met; I was quite satisfied. I was there for a few years before I noticed that my legs were not as strong as they had been when climbing stairs, and I felt unwell for parts of the day. If I had a bite to eat, however, that feeling of nausea would pass, so I made a habit of having a mid morning snack.

When I explained my physical issues to my doctor, he suggested I start by taking some iron to see if that made a difference. After about three months, though, he decided that low iron wasn't the problem, so I had blood work every couple of months. After the first incident—my fall—I'd been diagnosed with fibromyalgia. The doctor ran with that thought and said that since most professionals were not yet entirely familiar with the diagnosis of fibromyalgia, my current issues could be connected to that.

Meanwhile, I was not feeling well at all. I kept working through the pain and hoped the tests would reveal an answer. After about six months, I realized that the doctor had never tested a urine sample, and since the problem was affecting me with a burning sensation, I took it upon myself to take a sample on my next visit. I explained why I brought it, although I had mentioned the symptom earlier, and the doctor treated me for a yeast infection. Now, he said he would test the sample.

When he returned a few moments later, he looked angry. I thought he was angry at me, but he said, "Your blood sugar level is nineteen. You have diabetes." He also sounded angry as he proceeded to give me a prescription for Metformin. He told me how to take the medication and said I should come back in three months. I felt my condition was somehow my fault.

Over those three months, the Metformin worked, and at my next doctor visit, he apologized for his tone of voice the last time I'd seen him. "I wasn't angry with you," he said, "but with myself for not finding the cause sooner."

I had noticed that he seemed to be forgetful. He'd been my family doctor for over thirty years, so maybe he was getting too old to still be in practice. Shortly after that, he retired, and I felt bad. He was a terrific doctor, and I was lucky to have him for all those years. He did not err often over the years, and I trusted him.

I continued working at that company for about eighteen months. My general health was deteriorating, and my legs remained weak I was having a lot of joint pain, trouble sleeping, and sleep apnea, for which I was using a CPAP machine. I had trouble walking more than a few feet at a time. I sat at my job, so other than getting in and out of the office, I could tolerate the pain with my medications. Then the lethargy and chest pressure started. I didn't say anything about it for a while. I had my first appointment with my new doctor, and he put me on sick leave. He sent me for tests, but because the results either were okay or inconclusive, he treated me as he saw fit. I thought, *At least there's nothing seriously wrong*, but I had to stay off work. The chest pain became more pronounced. Walking or climbing stairs was simply too hard.

I received short-term disability for a while. Then one day, about two or three months in, I received a letter saying I no longer met the criteria for disability insurance. Of course I phoned the insurance company and asked them to explain. They didn't tell me any more than they had in the letter—that they had reviewed my file and decided I no longer qualified, according to their new policy. *This is just great*, I thought. *How is a person supposed to survive?* I had chills; I was so upset that I was going to lose my only source of income and not be able to get by. It was a dreadful realization.

The following morning I called a lawyer, who agreed to look into it for me. When he called a few days later, he told me the insurance company had dropped coverage on several other people for the same reason—their policy had changed.

"How can this be?" I asked him. "I originally was eligible."

"This sort of thing is not unusual," he explained. "Insurance companies do this once in a while because so few will go after them to recover payments—they can't afford the cost of lawyers and court procedures. They may get sued by one or two, but in the end they come out ahead because they no longer have to pay the others they cut."

I could not believe my ears. "I will go after my payments regardless," I told him. "It isn't right to do this to people. Bread winners, single parents, people who have no one else—this isn't fair. Even though I've paid into the insurance at work, they still did this."

It was a matter of integrity. I decided that even if I went broke, I had to fight. Why did they sell insurance? Most of us buy insurance so we can feel protected. We feel more secure, knowing we have insurance on which we can rely. To realize it doesn't always work out that way is frightening. We don't know how they will react if we put in claims. We need a regulating agent to protect us from that sort of fraud.

So the expensive drawn-out process began. Mine was not a

contingency lawyer, so I was obligated to pay retainers as I started the lawsuit—thousands of dollars in the beginning and then incremental payments. If I won my lawyer would get around a third of the settlement. By this point, though, I was committed to going ahead with the claim. In the end, regardless of the result, I would know I'd fought for the principal. I hoped to at least feel the satisfaction of doing the right thing and standing up for my rights. If I lost, I would have to deal with it then. It was expensive, and I had no way of paying at that time. If I lost, I probably would have to make payments for the rest of my life.

If someone had told me how conniving the insurance company would be, I wouldn't have believed it. I do not have any respect for insurance companies. I've heard that automobile insurers are the same; they charge as much as they can, and it always seems to be enough to strain the buyer's wallet. It doesn't look like we will be getting breaks there any time soon. They insist their rates have to be high because of false claims. They assume we will be filing false claims so we must pay up front. They charge a lot in the beginning, and if you need to make a claim, there are deductibles to pay.

I have spoken to many people who have had nightmare problems with insurance companies. It seems they question legitimate claims to the nth degree. I think in the long run, they don't ever intend to pay. When they sell us the policy, they don't want to see a claim, legitimate or not.

Chapter 6

WHO CAN WE TRUST?

This was my second claim and second rejection. It was a different insurance company than with the first claim, so I wondered if this was standard procedure. I asked around if anyone had problems with insurance claims. It seemed it wasn't unusual to have to fight for your claim and prove you're entitled to it. There seemed to be no recourse for me.

After about four years, I received notification from my lawyer that the insurance company had hired private detectives to follow me around to see if they could film me doing anything I shouldn't be doing with what I claimed to have wrong with me. They even took videos through the front windows of my home and followed me into a movie theater.

The movie was related to the grieving process. My husband had just passed away, and I was grieving. My grief counselor recommended the movie to me. Finding out about detectives invading my privacy depressed me to the point where I felt like dropping the claim. I could not cope, and I doubted the advice anyone gave me. I thought no one really understood how degraded I felt not to be believed and thought of as having filed a fraudulent claim.

The thought of detectives sneaking around behind me as they would follow a criminal—I could not be consoled. I saw a psychiatrist who helped me to understand the situation. As time passed, I realized I was falling into the insurance company's trap. Soon afterward, things seemed to ease up, and I was able to develop a more positive attitude. I knew I was doing the right thing. I was being honest and would stand my ground, no matter what.

I did see the detectives once or twice. My daughter said she'd noticed a couple of men sitting in a car across the road from my house. My son put it into perspective when he asked what I'd done that I was worried they'd filmed it. I hadn't done anything out of the ordinary, and I wasn't well enough to go anywhere. But it was an invasion of my privacy, and it was hard to think of them filming me. After discussing it with my children, I saw it as intimidation and was able to look at the situation differently. I realized I wasn't the only one who was treated this way; it was probably their standard procedure, and others had to deal with them too. I didn't make it right, but I didn't feel so isolated.

My lawyer said if I quit, then the company would win. I thought, *Oh no they don't, not without a fight*, and I carried on the rest of the battle with renewed gusto. I was determined to prove to them that not everyone is out to cheat the system. As a matter of fact, most people are not. It is the insurance companies' mind-set that is telling. If they think clients are not ill, then all the doctors, specialists, and hospital technicians who treat those clients also must be dishonest for saying there is indeed something wrong. After all, the insurance company requires medical reports from several sources on an ongoing basis.

That is why I am led to believe the insurance companies only want the money we pay to have insurance, but they don't seem to want to pay any claims. They should be investigated themselves and action taken to make them comply with the laws that protect the public from this kind of harassment. If people have multiple health issues, they are in for a grueling time to convince their insurers, who tend to think the people are hypochondriacs or flatly abusing the system.

I do assume there are laws to protect us.

Chapter 7

SHAMEFUL BEHAVIOR

I wonder why we never hear of lawyers or insurance companies being charged by the law. Perhaps the media simply doesn't report it, but it's not like them to overlook such news. Surely there are dishonest insurance companies and lawyers. How does the law deal with them? I've heard there are criminal elements in both professions. I recently saw a television show that discussed this very thing—a well-known lawyer left town with his clients' money and moved to South Africa, where he could not be extradited.

Then there was a person who went into the money-lending business, and he lost his clients' money after making bad investments. According to the program, upon leaving town he wrote his clients an apology note, explaining what had happened and that they shouldn't expect their money back. I guess he is gone forever too. The program indicated it was hard to charge lawyers because they would claim they had made bad investments for their clients and had lost the money that way. Apparently, that is a difficult claim to prove. I imagine that anyone who invests years in education won't want to mess it up. Perhaps there is a benefit to having all that knowledge.

Lawyers are being investigated for overcharging by a firm in the United States. If you complain, they will look into it, apparently for any amount over ten thousand dollars. It is a firm that advertises on television. I do think that might make a difference.

I wonder if it is difficult to catch people in the insurance business who cheat as well. That could explain why some keep doing it. Of course, insurance companies have lawyers on staff to advise them. Perhaps there could be a law or two introduced to curb that type of behavior in the first place.

Maybe instead of stopping teenagers and young people on the street for misdemeanor charges, officers could be better assigned to finding white-collar criminals who affect many people in society. Their crimes take unsuspecting investors' life-savings. I would guess that it's a different departmental responsibility for fraud crimes. Either way, there must be a real shortage of officers. That should be of the highest priority in any city's budget, similar to the plight of health care workers. They probably could accomplish these goals if they were not chronically short-staffed. The police must be frustrated too. Bringing some of these high-class law breakers to justice would be a good start—those who take advantage of others by fraud.

With the escalating gun violence, law enforcement has their work cut out for them. We can't fault them for not tracking down or putting as much effort into finding white-collar criminals as they do those who commit crimes and killings on the streets. It all needs to be stopped somehow. It seems that no one knows the answers. One thing is certain: we have to wonder where all this violence and crime will lead us. Every time we need to have more officers in the police force, why is there never enough money in the budget? How do they even know where to begin each day? It would appear that the level of urgency would dictate the need to come up with the funding. Does it make sense that the level of poverty has something to do with the increase in violent crime? Even if there are no financial means for law enforcement to concentrate on white-collar crime, it's not right for lawyers and financial giants to take advantage of the unsuspecting public.

Do people who are higher up the corporate ladder have to

deal with this kind of bullying when they have a claim? I think probably not. Maybe it's a technique used on the average lower-income earners only because we are so vulnerable. I suspect this is the case because almost all those people with whom I spoke are in the lower-income wage bracket. It seems as though poor people have more trouble convincing the authorities that a crime was committed against them in the first place. Why is that? Is it their appearance? Is it because they don't look prosperous? Perhaps it's because the insurance companies and lawyers think those in a lower-income bracket don't have the money to go through the court proceedings and be successful. Getting into the lower-class category is a gradual progression. It gets worse as the wages get lower and the prices go up. That's not hard to figure out, but why is it allowed to go on without taking steps to halt it before it reaches this level, where so many are suffering?

Surely there could be limits put on pricing markups and fees with professionals, just like there are with minimum wages. There are limits on the lower class for wages, but the corporations and wealthy businesses are able to slip by unnoticed by the tax department. They can hide their money offshore, and they don't seem to draw anyone's attention to the problem. They make the lower-class crime look like minor offenses compared to the money they play around with. How is this legal?

Chapter 8

TAKING ADVANTAGE

In the end, I won my lawsuit, but it really was about my missed wages. I struggled for a long time until I was offered the settlement. I owed a lot of money to the people from whom I borrowed—my relatives and friends. After waiting for almost nine years (I think they wanted me to disappear so they wouldn't have to deal with me), it was a sad victory for me. Although I finally settled with them, I didn't feel vindicated, not by any stretch of the imagination. After all was said and done, it was money they'd owed me in the first place. I may appear weak to some, but not everyone is equipped to mentally deal with a situation like this, and I'm sure the insurance companies depend on that—people drop the lawsuit in the early stages, and the insurance companies end up winning without a battle. I know I felt intimidated.

I often think how I should have responded, but twenty-twenty hindsight doesn't come first. I should have demanded more attention from my lawyer. In the end, I was surprised by how little contact I had with him during the negotiations. He hardly ever called to discuss anything with me, and when I called him, he always kept the conversation short. Sometimes I wondered whose side he was on. The lawyer made out very well by the time he was finished with my case. I understand how they work—big education makes big bucks. They do have the advantage over their clients, and they use it.

In the end, it was just a waiting game to see who could outlast the other—the insurance company or me. It's important to be patient as you wait and wait. The lawyers seem to be equipped with excellent waiting skills. Lawyers have full advantage over their clients. They have seen this scenario many times before and know how to play their game. It would be helpful if they explained it to their clients from the start. That is why I wonder which one they are representing sometimes.

I think my lawyer could have spent much more time with me, explaining how to proceed in the beginning. If you are going through a similar experience, don't hesitate to ask questions and demand answers. That is where I made my mistake, assuming my lawyer would automatically tell me all I needed to know. That was not the case. Unfortunately, we usually don't realize that we have been treated unfairly or overcharged until the deal is done. Then we already have signed off with the company or lawyer involved. At that point, there seems to be no recourse for the victim.

People not being able to bring these companies to justice financially is just another way low-income families pay because of their lack of funds. There seem to be lots of ways for the companies to take advantage of them. In my case, after all their threats, they ended up settling out of court. That told me they'd been trying to intimidate me all along so I would give in and quit the battle—and I almost did. Insurance companies do not need to do that to people who are trying to make a living. They would probably not take so many liberties if there were stiffer penalties on them.

Some people try to beat the system, but why not check on them before cutting off life-altering wages for legitimate claims. Maybe a lie detector test would help. It seems to work for the law and would be easier on the innocent victims. Then charge them if there is a problem. If the authorities can track murderers and other criminals through their knowledge, why can't they find these people in the same way? This appears to be criminal behavior that the insurance companies use to intimidate the average person into believing he or she is the one doing wrong. It's all a mind game. There must be guidelines in place for that kind of thing, so they can't just do as they wish. We mere mortals have rules to follow in this world; why not them?

Why not put into place a rule or two to protect us against them? If that is how the law works, maybe it's time for serious reviews of these methods. If the companies are doing this within the law, it is despicable. I assume that most people are honest, but it appears that the insurance companies assume that their clients are dishonest. The business world, in most cases, uses our ignorance to its advantage— at least some in business.

How many insured people try to commit fraud against these companies? Why is that their only defense with an insurance claim? We do not need anyone degrading us like that. We expect others to treat us with respect unless they are given reason not to do so. If they don't, it seems like bullying to me.

That is lesson number two: be prepared to fight for your rights and recognize when to do it.

Chapter 9

A REASON TO COMPLAIN

Another bee in my bonnet involves emergency rooms. A few years ago I had discomfort in my chest, and over time I became short of breath. This went on for a few weeks. One day when it was particularly bad, my daughter took me to the emergency room at our local hospital. I registered at triage, and they told me to have a seat in the waiting room. Soon after, they called me in to take blood and then sent me back to the waiting room. We waited for over four hours.

Finally, I said to my daughter, "If something was seriously wrong, they would have called me by now." I pointed to a sign in the waiting room. "That says they proceed by severity. I'm ready to leave now."

Just then they called me to the emergency room desk, and then they could not get me in a bed fast enough. They even took another patient out of the bed, saying they needed the bed for me because I was having a heart attack. This was four and a half hours after I arrived. I thought, *I could be dead by now.* The doctor inserted a stent, and I was kept in the hospital for about three weeks.

No one ever explained what took so long to get the results of my blood test; they carried on as if that was proper procedure. After I went home, I did not feel 100 percent well, but I was somewhat better. Then, eighteen months later, I had a more severe heart attack. When I went to the emergency room on this occasion, I butted in the line and told them I was having a heart attack. The triage nurse recognized me and got me help right away. They told me later that probably saved my life. After another few days I went home with another stent, feeling much better this time. What a difference! I had lots more energy, and I could not believe how much more I could accomplish. The irony is that I even survived the first attack, even though I received great service the second time. When dealing with life-threatening emergencies, I'd expect up-to-date technology to be readily available every time.

After that I did have more of a normal life and felt much happier within myself. I felt good for about seven more years before illness struck me again. This time it was a stroke. That Saturday morning in January, I was going downstairs to do my laundry when I noticed my right foot would not turn on the landing. I laughed and thought, *This is weird.* I tried to move it, but it would not lift off the floor. I realized it was probably not a simple thing, and I thought about a stroke after a minute but brushed it off. It really seemed too minor to be serious—I can see how someone would dismiss it as unimportant—but I knew I should go to the hospital emergency again and let the doctors tell me it was nothing to worry about.

This time they checked me and had me do certain movements with my face, hands, and body. They did some blood work, which showed I was not having a stroke. After spending six hours at the hospital, I was told to go home but to come back if it got worse.

I did not even get home. It was about half an hour later when my face and hand would not move, so I returned to the hospital. A doctor came right away and informed me that I was having a stroke.

"The doctor who was here earlier sent me home half an hour ago and told me I was not having a stroke," I said.

"I've just come on duty," he said, "so I didn't see you the first time, but you've missed the window of opportunity to have the clot-busting procedure."

I was actually at the hospital within the time frame necessary for the procedure—within the first half hour of the stroke symptom—so *they* missed the window, not me. In the end, however, the neurologist said that with my other problems I would not have been a candidate for the clot-busting procedure.

I was admitted and spent the next seven weeks in the hospital for treatment and rehab; then I attended outpatient rehab for about eight weeks or so. I'd had a brain stem stroke and survived it with right-side damage. I worked very hard at strengthening exercises, and I still do. Most people say I have made an amazing recovery. I agree. I still function fairly well and enjoy my family immensely. It made me realize what is important in this world.

You have to hold your loved ones near, and let them know what they mean to you—that they are your life's dreams. You just never know what's around the corner. I feel blessed to be living in this time because when my grandfather had a stroke in the 1950s, they did not know as much about strokes as they do now. He lay in a nursing home for eleven years.

For the first ten years, we thought he was unresponsive and couldn't hear us talking. When my grandmother died, however, we went to visit my grandfather after her funeral. He struggled to lift his hand to his mouth and blow a kiss up to heaven. We were shocked to see that. Up until then, we'd never seen him move. It was a life lesson for us and a touching experience.

I don't want anyone to think I have no clear reason for feeling the way I do about medical issues. Here's another situation that occurred. On a stormy night in December 2015, my nephew was in a car accident on his way home from work—his car hydroplaned into oncoming traffic. He survived but was left a paraplegic with breathing problems. He was in the best hospital in Ontario, Canada, for his type of injuries and received excellent care. After six months or so, he his breathing improved, but he still needed monitoring. He wasn't healed by any means. The doctors decided to move him to a different floor. Although they didn't give a reason, I think it was because they needed the bed in critical care.

He was on the new floor for a few days when he had an incident with his breathing, so they took him back to the original floor for closer monitoring. A few days later, he seemed to be improving so he was moved upstairs again. He was stable and improving slowly but steadily. We were thrilled that he was finally making progress. The plan was to transfer him to a rehab center to complete his recovery when he was able to breathe on his own.

Then in August, when he apparently was not being watched as closely as usual because the staff was busy, he choked and stopped breathing. Unfortunately, the nurses did not find him soon enough; he could not be revived. Our family feels that his demise was a direct result of a nursing shortage and not the fault of anyone on staff.

This is truly a heartbreaking situation and does not need to be. Surely hospitals can find other ways to save money. People suffer— and die—for the sake of a few dollars. Critically ill patients lie on gurneys in the hallways of hospitals, waiting to be admitted, sometimes for days at a time. My brother recently was taken to the emergency room. They didn't have a bed for him, so he lay in the hall for two and a half weeks. His family stayed overnight to care for him around the clock. The hospital finally moved him up to palliative care, but he died later that day. Is this any way to treat the ill?

I'm sure the people in charge of health care in Ontario would not want this to happen to their families, so let's see some drastic changes in that area. Lip service does not fix the problems. Sometimes the very people we elected into office are the ones who think they can ignore us. There is no way we are being fooled. We know there should be priorities in government spending. Health care is nothing to play around with and should never be used as a bargaining tool— not ever.

Chapter 10

THE UNFAIRNESS REACHES US ALL

There is a major problem with hospital and doctor's office parking lot fees. Do the dignitaries have to pay? I think probably not. There seem to be different laws for the dignitaries.

Why would anyone try to make a profit by taking advantage of someone who is ill? We don't get sick or hurt or have emergencies on purpose, so why don't they give everyone a break and cut the fares altogether as a gesture of good will. When I think about how things are going, it seems that someone is purposely dreaming up ways to make us pay more and more, while telling us it's a necessity for us, that it's the only way to raise enough revenue to keep the country running smoothly. It all sounds like someone is not spending his allowance on the right things. It seems that no matter what we have to pay, nothing ever gets any better. Before you know it, they are asking for more for something else.

We have already paid our taxes. Use them appropriately, and do not squander them on frivolous things, as Momma used to say.

Paying to park at a hospital is just not right.

It seems as if cities and municipalities continue to find more ways to keep us paying. Once it is approved, the prices go up and up until it gets ridiculous.

I have talked to a lot of senior citizens who are living on a fixed income, They have expressed how hard it is to pay for parking, sometimes for long hospital stays for the elderly. One older lady had a sad story. She told me her husband had been in the hospital for a long time and would not be getting out any time soon. She was in tears because she could only afford see him twice a week because she could not afford the parking fees. That is very unsettling to me. Here is a couple who have worked in Canada all their lives and contributed to the Ontario economy, and this is how they are treated at this stage of their lives.

They were the builders of our country, and if this seems right, then there is something wrong with us. They absolutely deserve better. They have earned it. Again, we have these charges to help, but it does not appear to be helping. The hospitals still have beds they can't use because of staffing cuts. Does this make sense? I suppose some hospitals have all their beds in use. It doesn't change the fact that going to the emergency room at most hospitals can be a very long, expensive day.

When I had to look into a problem we had with a ticket at our local hospital, I had to call British Columbia to take care of it because that is where they were based. That says to me that the money we pay does not even benefit our own province, let alone our hospital. How are we to change these situations? The only thing we can do is let the right people know how we feel and hope they will fix it for us. They are our representatives in government, and we have to depend on them to do the right thing for us.

Without solid opportunities for work and pay raises to match the cost of living, it will continue to get harder until we simply can't manage any more. A lot of people are at that point now, and no one has any solutions for the near future. And that is my point—the help needs to come soon. People are desperate, right now, today. If you look around, you can't help but notice them.

When another election looms, there will be promises as there always are, but just like in the past, we can't rely on those promises coming to fruition after the election. The new party doesn't seem to know what they are getting into until they are elected. It seems the situation from the last party in office is always a shock to them, and they have to try to sort it out. We are led to believe it's hard to do anything productive for the public in the beginning of their terms. It takes time for the transition, but we expect to see those positive changes after the transition period. It doesn't always happen that way. Why?

As of this writing, there is another election next year, and we already are hearing the usual promises. Someone really wants to get in there, it seems. If only it would happen like candidates are saying now, but it never does, if past promises are any indication.

Blaming anyone is not useful. They all say they are trying, and we have to listen. It must be a daunting and overwhelming task. I suspect very few relish the idea of being in power in this upheaval today. It never seems to slow down for us to take a breath. The pace is so fast, and countries can't find a common ground. Everyone is trying to sort out his or her own space; others are accused of interfering; and tempers get short. It's like they need a big time-out.

Canada can relax, however, with regard to our ability to understand that our elected officials are working to make things better. Our country has worked for world peace without getting much credit, but we don't need to be told; we know. We have a good reputation among other countries, and our government and military have earned praise over many years. We have a lot to be proud of and can hold our heads high.

Chapter 11

THE PHARMACEUTICAL CONUNDRUM

What about prescription drugs? It's simple enough for the doctor to prescribe what we need, but the issue lies in getting the pharmacy to fill it with the brand name drug. Many times I have picked up my medicines only to discover they have filled the prescription with the generic form that I do not want. I have to tell them, "I would like the brand name, please."

"Oh, this is the same thing, and it's cheaper for you," the pharmacist says.

"I don't mind paying the extra money for the brand name," I say.

"You don't need to pay more for the brand name," the pharmacist insists. "It's the same."

"No, I don't want it," I say. "I want the brand name that my doctor prescribed."

"Well, this is already made up. Just take it."

That conversation is typical for the situation. In reality, why should the pharmacy care which one we prefer? Why does it make any difference to them? It makes no sense to me for them to argue with me. It shouldn't affect them either way.

I do not believe that the brand name drug and the generic are the same. If they are, then why is one so much cheaper than the other? I think the pharmaceutical companies are running the whole show. It seems they control the medical and pharmaceutical process. When did they get all the power? My common sense tells me that someone in a responsible position should monitor what is happening and is allowing pharmaceutical companies to overcharge and manipulate the consumers. In this country, they should answer to the health minister. Why are they getting away with this when they have rules to follow?

The markup on some medications is too high. Passing or enforcing legislation on the pharmaceutical companies probably would solve a lot or at least lessen the pain for a lot of folks. Take the epipen, for example. Why is it so expensive when so many people need to carry it? Drugs are discovered that work for different illnesses, and then they are priced out of the market. What's this about? Why does the government let them do this? Do they care for the sick, or is it only about money? Do the drug companies fund any major research to justify their larger and larger profits?

I think they could not care less about the public, and it's all about profit. Just take a look at the money they put into advertising. When watching their advertisements, listen to the side effects of some of these drugs. If your illness doesn't kill you, the drugs just might. More than once my druggist has told me not to take a particular drug because it should not be mixed with another one I'm taking. Sometimes when a person sees a number of different doctors for various illnesses, a mix-up can occur. The pharmacist will then call the doctor's office and straighten it out. I'm glad he's there to watch out for my health; at least he cares—I think.

I heard something interesting on TV recently about Australia; they only pay five dollars per prescription, and it is government-controlled. Doesn't that sound worth looking into? Apparently, it has been several years since any updates have been made to health care and drug-dispensing methods in Canada. How much longer can we wait? We are asked to donate to research, and then, when they manufacture a drug, we can't afford to buy it. What's the point? We have to survive paying charges for this and for that on all the bills and transactions we pay each month. There are so many additional charges now. Where did those come from, and who dreamed them up and approved them? Maybe these companies are lining their pockets and/or supporting their CEO's lifestyles while the working poor have to scrounge for their own existence. It isn't funny to those who have to live that way. Why don't these serious problems get recognized and dealt with? Why do they linger? How about someone stepping forward and answering some of these questions for us?

We certainly have a right to know what is going on in politics in our province. It seems as though we get as little information as possible. We need to know why things are going the way they are. We pay taxes, and they are not cheap, but it should earn us the right to an explanation.

We are not the ones hiding our money in tax-free lands.

With all the struggles and heartache we have to endure through serious illness in our families (they seem more prevalent now than in past years), this should be the first thing on Ottawa's agenda. Why are we ignored at a time when everything in our province seems to have become crucial and needs attention? If we can see it, elected officials must too. If they don't, I have a message for them: see what needs attention before more people lose their heat, food, and homes. Please listen to your constituents and help in some way. We are depending on your promises to improve our world. So far no one seems to be benefiting from those heartfelt promises you made to us when you wanted our votes to get into office. The ball is in your court. Make that difference for us so we can begin to relax a little and live with less stress. It will never become totally stress-free, but a little leeway in our lives would help.

Maybe someone could explain why it is so beneficial to be elected into office. So many politicians complain how hard the job is, yet they fight over getting elected to do it. There must be perks. Maybe that's it. Politicians, we need you to make urgent decisions for us, the people. Please concentrate on us and correct the wrongs that have fallen upon us.

Perhaps we still have a few politicians who will try to keep their promises and make a difference for the people, who desperately need to have change in order to survive. The problems are the same all over the province and need serious attention. Please do something. We can't afford heat and electricity anymore; it's that simple. That is a necessity for every home, regardless of income. In what way do we not deserve heat and hydro as much as any other working person? Most families do not just ignore their debts; they are probably without an income or have another legitimate reason for falling behind, likely something beyond their control. They may be victims of circumstance, and it's probably temporary because of the economic situation in Ontario. The economy likely will pick up eventually, but in the meantime maybe a better temporary solution can be put in place for them.,

This hydro fix is really no solution at all. It is still far too expensive. How in the world is it going to help in the long run?

Chapter 12

THE FRUITS OF OUR LABOR

Some pensions are extravagant, and others provide very little to live on each month. It doesn't seem right that most seniors have to budget for the month very frugally. Perhaps they could be revised to a more realistic amount. That would be a step in the right direction. It might have been all right when things were rosy and the budget was balanced, but it does not seem all right now, not with the economy the way it is. We have had cutbacks, so maybe it is time for seniors to be considered for an increase that will help them, rather than a token amount, so they have some freedom in their golden years. Surely the seniors are not responsible for today's situation.

It is still a worry that many women are single parents and are not paid salaries equal to their male counterparts, even though it was promised years ago. Women are still making only 75–80 percent of male wages. How can this be, after all this time? Their children could suffer because of Mom's low wages.

How many issues do we need before the situation will be considered critical? Now is the time for action. Politicians probably don't want people protesting in the streets, and we citizens don't either; that's like airing your dirty laundry in public. Others don't need to know if it does not concern them. We need elected officials, however, to help us figure out some solutions. These issues have gotten out of hand, and a lot of residents are suffering the consequences of decisions made in the last few years. Are there plans to come to our aid any time soon?

Some of us cannot afford to take the medicines prescribed to keep us well. Is this the way we have should treat people in our province? Does anyone consider this fair? If you have been made aware of the situation, can you imagine the pain and the worry?

We are still waiting for change to help us survive and to be able to manage our households. How much longer will take? It certainly is not frivolous to expect to see improvement. If we can get the point across now, we will have succeeded. Maybe it will bring about some change, and we will all breathe easier.

Let your voice be heard.

After many years of seeing the way situations like this were handled a few years ago and comparing that to now, I believe some of the changes are just not good for us. Maybe some of it is our fault. Maybe we ask for so many promises that it is impossible to accomplish them all. The ones that affect livelihood and the basic necessities of life, however, must be looked at seriously and provided to us.

I'm not the only one feeling the pinch. It's apparent everywhere—in the daily news, in rundown areas, in the amount of crime and the severity of the crimes being committed, and in soaring prices. People are desperate to move on, but it's not possible right now. There is no way to get ahead without legislative changes to the identifiable unique problems. So many are stuck in the rut and cannot see their way out. It happened very gradually, as things tend to do, until we got to where we are.

We are affected negatively by decisions made by the people we put in power, expecting the opposite effect. It's time to resolve at least some of these issues. Who can support a family on fifteen dollars an hour? That is a very low minimum wage, but it doesn't come into effect until January 2018.

Life was supposed to get less stressful as we age, not more. I think the level of accomplishment for the future and getting through this time successfully is at an all-time low. It makes me feel defeated, and I'm scared for youngsters coming into the world at this time, with all the upheaval.

The health care system, employment, food additives, gun laws, discrimination, housing, household debt, intimidation, education— it goes on and on in almost every aspect of daily living. It all seems to be breaking up at once, and I can't help but wonder why it's happening now, at this time. It is not a good situation to leave for the next generation to resolve. It doesn't look any different, so why do we feel more vulnerable now than in the past? The only thing changing is the world around us.

If we can't get our affairs in order, there probably isn't much chance to compete in the global market. Everyone seems to be at each others throats right now, and some countries are walking on eggshells, not wanting to create a disturbance. Others are threatening with missiles. Things do not seem settled, as they were only a short time ago. It seems we need to check the world situation daily. My parents said that it was like that for a time before World War II.

This is very unsettling. With the weapons available now, I hope everyone in power thinks twice before pushing any buttons. There are so many ways to negotiate, these countries should try all of them first. I pray for that for our future generations. The last thing we need is some hothead in charge.

Chapter 13

HEALTH AND DAY CARE

We're seeing a lot more personal service (home care) workers now. That's good, but we have to consider that as much as we need them, they are not nurses. They are a tremendous help with everyday activities at home for the disabled—bathing, laundry, household chores, and just someone to look in and check on shut-ins. They are also a great help to working people who have to leave their parents home alone. Personal service workers (PSWs) can see that their patients take their medicine and eat properly. There is relief in knowing they will come on a regular basis to tend to elderly and ailing patients. We owe them a debt of gratitude.

A lot of seniors don't want to leave their homes for care, and PSWs are a blessing in that regard. A lot of families choose to nurse their loved ones at home, if possible. That is a wonderful solution for seniors, as nursing homes and long-care facilities are expensive and are facing problems. We have had some bad experiences in nursing homes in the past. It has made people think twice about leaving members of their families there.

Our lives have become so full, however, it is hard to manage home care. It puts a strain on everyday activities for all concerned. It is a selfless undertaking for the family. So much compassion is being shown to one another. The hard times draw us closer and work as a kind of equalizer for society. That can only lead to more caring, and that is definitely a good thing.

We still depend on professional medical people for health services. PSWs can only do so much, but it helps in a lot of ways and is a step in the right direction.

There also are problems with childrens day care centers now. Most have a waiting list and are expensive. This is another area that could use some updating. If we must spend most of our pay on child care, it defeats the purpose of going out to work. If a person has two, three, or four children in day care, is there a discount? Why can't a fair plan be worked out before introducing some of these day care facilities? Little thought seems to have gone into it before it was hurried through at the last minute.

There was an article on Facebook that discussed placing childrens day care at a retirement facility. Apparently, it went well. There might be new modern-day solutions to some of these old problems. Worth looking into, perhaps.

What is the long-range plan for the economy now? With employers requiring university degrees, will the job market be able to sustain these highly educated people? Will it pick up so much that there will be jobs for everyone, or is it going to be high unemployment, as it has been for the past twenty-five years or so? It takes a long time to pay back most education debt. If there are not going to be well-paying jobs available, what is the point? There must be big improvements in the work force if it is to prosper to the point of providing jobs for all who have university degrees. That seems to be the reality as of this writing. We need to have jobs with benefits again. That is another reason the money goes so fast. Paying for your own medication, dentists, and procedures that are not covered through work gets expensive.

Money is hard to come by and getting harder all the time. Maybe if we could get decent-paying jobs, it would make life better. The minimum wage is so low that some families are better off applying for welfare in order to survive. The work available now seems to be part-time or contract work. The cost of living is going up and up. And wages are not covering the cost. We would probably be better off bartering, like in the old days. It seems brilliant now, if you think about it—at least there was shelter and food.

Chapter 14

ALTERNATIVE LEARNING

Do you remember when we had promising apprenticeship programs and how they enhanced the workforce? It would not hurt to have a mandatory program like that for dropouts, youth, and newcomers to learn from the best. We had some very skilled workers come from that time.

Some people can do amazing work with their hands and be very productive. We could use them now. This shows that some people manage just as well without money for higher education. Some will apply themselves and still have success in life. Folks who do not have the money to attend universities could take advantage of apprenticeships and still have lives of independence and be proud contributing members of society. There are talented people who could pass on their common sense and knowledge to another generation. It will take them far in life as well. It doesn't always have to be book learning.

Why is a person required to have post secondary education in today's society? Most of us would like to see our children get a post secondary education, but some of us can't manage it financially. It is good to know there are wonderful alternatives and opportunities for education, even if it does not include university or college. No one should despair if he or she cannot attend university. There are also jobs for the skilled, as well as individual courses for specific jobs that do not require university. If you would like to work in a specific field, look into courses for adults at night schools that train for that particular career. It will be an eye-opener for a lot of adults to see what is available at a community college. It is a good alternative, and it will give a sense of achievement as well. Don't worry about your age. People of all ages are realizing the advantage they can gain by continuing their schooling, even with one or two specific courses.

Chapter 15

DIVERSITY

Young school children of different nationalities who are integrated in classrooms don't notice their differences. They are simply other children, and that is how they learn. Children come into the world full of innocence, and it will continue that way if no one interferes and teaches them differently. Prejudice is taught.

Their adult lives are produced through experiences, and any disregard for others is learned throughout life's journey. I can see a difference in childrens perception of one another now, as compared to when I was young. I think the difference is the melting pot. It is old hat to our children now and a normal, everyday occurrence. They accept one another, and diversity is just another word to them.

We have been accused of discrimination, but we have always welcomed newcomers; after all, we were once immigrants ourselves. We are all in this together, but a few bad apples can ruin the barrel. Sometimes frustration can lead to conflict between us. It's hard to deal with feeling unable to compete with others in society because we don't feel equal to them. Sometimes we feel inferior to those who have worked their way to a more comfortable position in life. Maybe we feel that we can't accomplish independence. There are many reasons, but I think most of us just need encouragement and confidence in our own abilities. We all have something unique about

41

us, and when we realize that almost all of us have our own fears, they're easier to overcome. There should be no worries about fitting in. Fears are a part of living, and we strive to face them. Conquering our fears makes us stronger.

When we find common ground—something we can take an interest in and work together on sharing our knowledge—it alleviates a lot of the fears about one another. Getting to know other individuals puts a different slant on our outlook. If we do that, it benefits us all. Try to find a way to help a person relax, even if it's only a friendly hello or gesture. Smiles can work wonders. It is surprising how receptive most people will be.

If we are supplied the tools to make an effort to accomplish anything, the sky is the limit. Most people want to be productive and will work for a living, given the opportunity.

I'm not criticizing anyone who is successful or has managed to do well financially. It would be a perfect world if that were the case for all of us. Striving for prosperity and inching toward it gives us a feeling of accomplishment. No one likes to be stuck in limbo. If we can get ahead, little by little, it urges us to push toward our goals.

The people who don't have jobs but are trying to do the right thing for their families are no less worthy than the wealthy. The problem is not what anyone thinks of us; it is how we perceive our situation when no matter how hard we try, things don't go right. After a while, it gets us down until it's hard not to think of it as being our fault. A "loser"—that term is used frequently. I suspect it's an expression used by the younger generation to tease one another, but I don't want us to think that way about ourselves. It is a sad time when people in positions to help others won't recognize them as people who need a little boost when they are struggling.

Chapter 16

OUR HOMELESS

Most homeless people are not there because they chose to be but because life has gotten them to this point. Do we care about them? Of course. Can they be helped? Of course. It seems, however, that they are the forgotten ones. Who can best help them? The government or municipalities?

How long will this go on before we see the real tragedy happening in our own provinces. Some have died, and more will perish if they are not taken care of and housed. Have a heart, politicians, and look after your political area. Please do your job. That's all we can ask. If you were to ask what to spend our taxes on, homelessness and poverty would be a great beginning.

Some restaurant and cafe owners in Toronto have very generously decided to offer the poor free lunches, coffee, and sandwiches on a daily basis. It would be lovely if others could get together and share that good deed among themselves and take turns periodically. What a wonderful gesture. Thank you for your kind hearts. This gesture may not seem like a big deal, but it is huge. Imagine if you were poor, cold, and hungry. What a difference it would make to you. It is a great beginning to do this for them. What if there were offers of vacant buildings where the homeless could settle? Ontario has a few empty buildings. If a big company could pay to heat them, it would be perfect. Why should the buildings sit empty when they could be used and perhaps save lives? Even without heat, they would provide shelter against the elements. It would be beneficial if the public could take care of the homeless, but they don't have the resources. Larger industries, politicians, and counselors could have it handled with ease.

With real estate prices rising beyond belief and other prices out of reach for so many, there is bound to be more homelessness. It would be tragic if we had more deaths attributed to homelessness. It is just a matter of time before it gets worse.

Where did this nonsense of home pricing start? It surely can't be the average Canadian. Who has hundreds of thousands of dollars for a home when they can't afford the necessities of life? Young people are moving from the downtown core to the outer regions of Ontario to find affordable housing and employment. It looks like it is a trend starting. Some of the young adults have to live with two or three others in cramped rental space to stay in the city to work. The rental spaces consist of very tiny spaces in some instances. Landlords charge astronomical rents for very little, and they get away with it. It is not an ideal situation to be cramped together with others at those outrageous rents. At least they should have the comfort of home for their efforts.

Chapter 17

THE CHILDREN

Crime and disrespect have always been with us, and we need not blame each other or the youngsters trying to mature to adulthood in this climate. It must be so hard for them to understand what is happening in our world. It is hard for us to understand, and we are supposed to be mature.

When people are depressed, things always seem darker, and perhaps crime seems to be their only solution. If you were desperate enough, would such thoughts seem the only logical way out? Most of us don't think that way, but there is no telling how a troubled mind would think.

People who actually care about our environment are trying to help by making change for the good. Some areas of the province have been developed, and that has made a positive difference to our landscape. It looks beautiful. Perhaps we need to stop beautification of the land for a while, however, and put some much-needed money into helping those who cannot manage to take care of themselves. We could give them the help and encouragement they need. The ones who break the laws of society cost the taxpayers so much money. It is ironic that the ones who commit these crimes against us get priority funding to stop them. Those who suffer quietly day by day get nothing for their aid.

It's not clear how we got to this point, but it reminds me of a time in grade school when we had a competition, and everyone wanted to win—to the point of cheating to achieve that win. As adults, it seems that need to be the best still is in some of us. Unfortunately, some people want to make money by taking advantage of the less fortunate. It's not child's play anymore; it's time to grow up and be responsible, contributing adults who consider their fellow adults as equals. Taking advantage of them is like stealing, and it still hurts to feel used by others. It's time to stop the pain and start the healing because some day we won't be able to fix this mess, and more people, especially our youngsters, will be hurt.

Chapter 18

NOW WHO IS BEING FOOLED

Some food companies are making the containers smaller and charging more money for their products. Almost every item we buy has gone up in price, and a lot of us do not even get cost-of-living raises. I heard on the news that some large retail outlets were charged with false advertising because they raised their regular price on items and then marked them down again, leading consumers to think they were getting a better price when it actually was the original price. Why do big companies do this to us? Some of the same stores have been fined previously as well. I assume they can afford to pay the fine, and so they do it again. Maybe their fines need to be higher.

Do these companies think we fell off the turnip truck on our heads? We need someone to be our watchdog. We've seen it before, and we'll see it again. Why do they think it's okay to do it to us, the very people who made them what they are today? Don't these large companies feel guilty? Do they think it's something we owe them? Please don't think you're fooling us; we know what's happening.

Most of us are so confused about our present-day world that we don't know where to begin. I have had many conversations with friends and colleagues who feel the same about the changing atmosphere and do not know how to deal with it. Striking up a conversation with people, wherever I happen to be, usually ends up with a discussion of how hard it is to get by. Maybe politicians should specify an address where people who have questions can write to them. It might be beneficial for us to have citizen representatives from various areas meet a couple of times a year with politicians to exchange ideas and discuss current problems.

It is not a total fix to the problems facing us, but it could bring to light some issues that need attention. Ontario is a huge province, and many things may get over looked because of topics that need to be addressed on a daily basis. Of course. it makes a lot of citizens think they are being ignored, when actually it could be a matter of priorities. A calm and productive get-together would be nice once in a while.

We need to heal and have the confidence that we can survive a real crisis. I may seem like an alarmist to some, but when average working-class parents and taxpayers do not feel their real situations are being dealt with appropriately, it is very worrisome and alarming indeed. It only says to these people that we are not heard. It is not to our advantage to keep quiet. Are we going to be included in the strategy for our province, or will things remain the same?

Some of us can't pay the rent, buy enough groceries, or pay debts on time, if at all. What kind of decision making is it when a person has to decide between paying a utility bill, buying groceries, or paying the mortgage or rent? Some get by for a while by selling off their possessions. They constantly dwell on the fact that they are not pleasing anyone because of their lack of funds. There just isn't enough to live on, and there is no indication that relief will come any day soon. This is a reason to worry. Most of us do not like what is going on, but we can't stop it without changes.

What if we get sick and need to go to the hospital or need medication we can't afford? It is downright frightening to think about it. Some have the impression they are not considered a contributing member of society if they are not gainfully employed. It might seem they are being left out, and the decisions for change should apply only to the prosperous.

Chapter 19

LETS WORK TOGETHER

We need to take strong action to get our representatives to pay heed to our plight. Just how to do that troubles me. I had to follow my heart and put my thoughts down on paper. If we can get someone to notice, it will be worth the effort. I have thought about our situation for a long, long time and now realize that it's not enough to only think about it. Someone needs to notice that things have to change.

I don't consider myself a writer, but if writing this book is what has to be done to get some recognition, I will do it, and I pray that the powers that be will listen. I want these problems to go away, and I am very worried for our little ones and young people. I hate to think what may happen if we don't act now. I believe my heart is in the right place—my dad used to say that.

Working together might help if all communities are represented and committed to the cause, and they join forces. With some government involvement, we would get a lot farther along; in fact, I see that as the only way to solve our concerns.

We all have felt defeat at some time in our lives, some more than others. It seems the fewer resources we have, the more often we are defeated, yet most of us opt not to seek help. We may be made to feel less worthy by those people whose job it is to help us. Some of us may have a more positive attitude in these types of situations. I wish I was more like that, but I'm not. I find it hard to relate to those who are not my equal.

I was in that situation more than a few times while struggling to raise my children, sometimes working two jobs to make ends meet. Although woman did not go out to work as much as they do now, I felt the need, early on in my marriage, to contribute financially. We got short on supplies now and then, but with the help of good friends, we never actually went without necessities. Many a night and for years at Christmas, I stayed up, unable to rest, not knowing how I would handle the next crisis. I just kept my faith and worked more hours, if I could, or got a part-time job over the stressful period. I did what I could, financially.

I was not afraid to fight for my beliefs, and I have learned to put up a good argument for my cause. I'm no longer intimidated; I've learned to be strong. I found out early on that it was my way to survival. I was fortunate because it was a bit simpler when my children were young to make an occasion great for them, before the advancements in electronics. Adults didn't spend money on themselves as much as they do now, and the holidays were for the children, especially Christmas. I don't know how young families manage these days. Keeping up with the Jones has taken on new meaning.

It sometimes was difficult for a large family to meet their obligations back then, but it's hard for a small family these days, and some simply can't manage. It's impossible to keep up with the changes.

Years ago, I never entertained the possibility of assistance. I was taught by the old saying "You've made your bed; now lie in it." Assistance was not as necessary or as available as it is today. It has since become a necessity, however, for many to exist. Those who live on credit find it impossible to come out on top. Credit now is the only way for some to simply survive. Who would have thought this would evolve into mass debt a few years down the road? Who thought through this credit card thing before introducing it to society? I'll bet those at the top had some idea of what was to come. It takes out the middle class altogether. Now who is suffering? You and me, the low-income people. Even though some of us did not start out in the low-income bracket, that's where we find ourselves because of the economy.

Also, those who take advantage of the public for personal gain have contributed to our downward slide and have added to the problem. We are aware of what is happening to us. Now we are in a situation of high debt with no certain means of getting out without help from the experts. The advice I've heard from lawyers and economists is to pay down your bills as much and as fast as you can, and find a money manager to help you. That is not really a viable solution for those without the money to pay in the first place. Again, it sounds like a solution for the more prosperous.

Now you can gamble with your credit card—that's not a good idea. The government does tell us to stay within our means, but that's hard to do when you have no money. Some are hoping to win their way out of debt. Most people realize you cannot win against the casino, but in desperation they think it's worth a try. A few years ago I did gamble, and once in a while I did win a bit, but I never got rich, of course. It was when I had steady employment, so I didn't suffer financially, but I would have been better off without it. I quit gambling after a substantial win, and I'm not sorry I did. People often get into a kind of cycle and become addicted to gambling, even though it doesn't seem so bad while they are doing it.

I actually started out innocently enough, an evening out here and there, but before I knew it, I was having more nights out. My gambling habit was bingo. Later on, I realized the cost to my livelihood. It seems as though credit-card and homeowner debts and extreme prices were approved by government beforehand; if not, they would have taken some action against it.

Are there solutions we don't know about yet? How are we going to get ourselves out? Heaven help us!

Payday loan places have popped up all over, and they generally have a very high interest rate—something else to get us further in debt. There is just no end. We are supposed to think of these places as solutions, and I guess they are temporary fixes, but they add to the problem too. This is someone else taking advantage of the situation and seems to be another way for a certain few to get rich because they don't feel bad taking advantage of people.

As soon as someone figures out how to take advantage of a situation, such as people with debt problems, it is not long before that type of business flourishes. Who finds such a business appealing? Of course it's the people with money problems. Here we go again.

Chapter 20

MAKE IT HAPPEN

We need better paying jobs. A lot of times families cannot survive on their incomes, and they struggle with two or sometimes three jobs to make ends meet. It is hard to get benefits anymore, with all the short hours and part-time employment, so if we are working two part-time jobs and have no benefits, we are no further ahead.

Childrens day care is so expensive, and there's often a waiting list for placement. Around and around it goes, from one obstacle to another. It's worrisome, not knowing from one day to the next what the outcome will be. Parents certainly didn't expect this to happen to their families. When day care was announced, it sounded great. Then when we found out it was too expensive, it seemed like a bad joke. But it is no joke. How are parents to deal with it?

Many companies have moved to foreign countries for cheaper labor, and that has had an impact on us. It must be hell for young people, educated or not, just starting out in the workforce.

How did that situation get so out of hand, and why isn't the government helping the people who need it to feed children who reportedly are starving by the thousands? Anyone who can make a difference should please do so. We have hungry, homeless children and adults here. Let's help our own to survive before giving to others. Charity begins at home. It only makes sense in a beautiful country like ours to eliminate the need. They seem to lack encouragement, friendship, food, housing, clothes, and probably even love. Let's show them caring about your fellow humans does still exist.

Someday maybe someone who is able will find an answer to this terrible housing problem we're living with—rundown apartments at astronomical rents and landlords who don't keep the buildings clean, let alone repaired. They expect renters to live in that squalor, yet they evict them for nonpayment of rent. Even if people go public with their problems, nothing seems to get done. Why aren't the laws enforced for this kind of behavior from landlords? We have a Landlord and Tenants Act. Why not get them going on these issues? These people are making victims of innocent renters who don't have any recourse because nobody listens. Nothing ever gets dealt with by the proper departments. It has been brought to their attention, but landlords frequently don't comply. Why is that? Shouldn't they be forced to correct the problems? Why are tenants living with bedbugs, cockroaches, mice and rats, or other vermin?

Repairs to appliances, plumbing, and the dwelling should be mandatory. Landlords who don't comply deserve to be punished. What's happening there? These people making our fellow humans suffer by bullying them into submission is lower than evil. They are not suitable for the positions they hold in society.

There is an ombudsman in Ottawa to contact for advice and for help with some of these problems, and he or she will look into individual circumstances. He or she is there to help the public.

If we can't give financial help, perhaps we can pick a family and donate clothing, food, or blankets. We could make a special occasion happy by giving a birthday gift or a Christmas dinner. Do what you can.

Chapter 21

TAKE NOTICE OF WHAT IS GOING ON

Every day we see TV ads that solicit money for everything from animals to sick children overseas, diseases, hospitals, or research. These are all good causes to which we might donate if we had the money, but we don't right now. Don't they realize people in this economy are strapped to the limit? When the good times turn bad, it is time to look after your own. We would like to be able to help others, and most of us have done so in the past, but we do have our own families to feed and take care of, with no or very little help at the moment.

It would be nice to be praised for our own successes and ability to be self-sufficient. Perhaps wealthy companies could help those causes (and get a healthy tax break too). After all, who made them wealthy?

What kind of information does the government keep about us? They sure seem to know a lot about our lives. Why can't they see who legitimately needs help, offer information on what the problem is right now, and give counseling to get people on the right track? From our viewpoint it seems like no one who has the power to change things cares or doesn't know how much we are affected by these problems.

Politicians come around to our doors during campaign time,

and they listen to us and say they will fix certain problems, but once they are voted into office, where do they go? Maybe on vacations on our bucks (or so I hear), but we do not question our representatives' behavior. We have that right as the electorate. Once in a while, it seems they make a scapegoat out of a few of their own to deter us from other troublesome doings in Parliament. Of course, that rumor goes around every time there is a scandal—it might be diversion. When there are complaints about politicians spending taxpayers' money on personal travel and expenses, I wonder what is really going on, though some of the accusations are too petty to worry about.

I believe traveling at taxpayers' expense has been going on for years. Most of it is legitimate, but we probably never will know to what extent. How exactly is the public supposed to react? What is all this secrecy? Some seem to think it's none of our business, but it's every bit our business, and we do have the right to know. After all, we—the taxpayers—pay their wages. We should know our financial situation. If their spending is what caused our problems, then it is really getting bad. Otherwise, it doesn't make much difference to us how they take their perks. We have real worries.

Chapter 22

CAN ORGANIC REALLY BE BETTER FOR YOU

Cancer, Alzheimer's disease, birth defects, autism—why are these diseases and conditions so prevalent in this advanced society? Do you suppose they are caused by the additives in food? Perhaps it's vitamin or weight-loss supplements we are told will make us live longer and be healthier, more popular, and less stressed.

Why do we have to buy "organic" food, which is grown without any additives or pollutants. What will the garden veggies and the meats and so on do to us? That is something I've wanted to know since organic produce was first introduced. Why would our food be contaminated in the first place? Is it a ploy to frighten us into spending more money to stay healthy? I recently saw on the news that certain veggies were marked organic when they were not, but the season was not so good for the growers, so the store just marked regular vegetables as organic at organic prices so they had something to fill their otherwise empty space.

If is the grocers wanted to keep that secret, they shouldn't have let the news media know about it. After all, once the public knows, they can't take it back. I do not watch the news daily, but I still manage to find out the odd thing that's happening. I wonder what organic is if it can be replaced with regular produce on a whim. It's not just an issue with organic foods—a company in Ontario was caught selling cheese as kosher that was not.

We might think that farmers are concerned about our health, and that's why they grow organic food. Maybe, though, it's another way we are being misled to spend more money at the supermarket. In the end, we can't tell the difference. We probably never will know if a genuine concern for consumers' health sparked this organic food era. We don't know if the food is any different until they put the "organic" sign on it. Maybe it's not.

A lot of us try to eat healthily because we don't want any of the diseases that seem so prevalent lately. Does it do us any good? Who knows? We used to take for granted that the food we purchased was good for us.

Some of the grocery items we buy all the time are not properly marked with all the ingredients in them. I thought there were laws to protect us from that. Apparently not. The manufacturers don't seem to be held responsible. The government says to read the label. Why would they tell us that if companies don't list the contents correctly? What is the reason for this?

We are being manipulated to make some companies richer than they already are. When are they going to get honest and let us live gracefully to the ends of our lives? We not going out of this world alive, and we would like to have some peace while we're still here.

There are problems in the funeral business as well. It has become so expensive for a funeral that more people are opting to have their loved ones cremated because it is more affordable. The government will pay up to twenty-five hundred dollars if you qualify. The actual burial cost can be ten times that. Is that necessary? You would think they would show a little compassion at a time like that. It is just another way to take advantage when we are most vulnerable.

It is like there's a new competition for duping the unsuspecting public.

We would like to be assured that our food, medicines, and

provinces are as safe as possible at any given time. Most of us strive to stay healthy. Knowing our government is doing their part would be very comforting. I know the FDA has rules. Enforcing the rules is the only way to guarantee food and drug safety. I imagine that some companies don't follow government regulations and hope they will not get caught. If they do, they can afford the fine.

If large companies want to change the world, why not help those who need it and quit taking advantage of us. We are asking for help ourselves, and it is a shame that greedy businesses are not happy with the profits they have. It's not enough, so they devised a way to get more.

How did they get this far without getting caught? It surely must be illegal. I don't think the average person would get away with it. Why are the companies any different?

We are living in an age where it is popular to make big money at anyone's expense. It has to be a big profit or else it's simply not good enough.

Chapter 23

TRUTH OR CONSEQUENCES

If we have been donating to the causes of the world for many years, why haven't things improved? The same goes for cancer cures and other horrible illnesses. I am sick of losing my beloved family members to cancer and heart disease, respiratory ailments, and poor management of health care services. Health care workers are expected to perform miracles when they are short-staffed; they can't save people single-handed. Why is the health care budget cut over and over? Is it because the government just doesn't care for us? It sure seems like it.

If everyone was as dedicated as most health care workers, we would all be better off. I have the feeling that the health minister would not have to abide by these rules if he or she became ill and needed medical attention. I think the rules would be waived for the health minister and his or her family. They would not have a problem with the system as we do. Every one of our lives is just as important as theirs. We need much better health care services.

I have heard years ago that there actually was a cure for some cancers, but whatever government was in power decided to snuff it because cancer was a way to balance the population. Sometimes I wonder, but it tells us that many years ago the same facts were being questioned. When we have relatives or friends who can't beat cancer and of course end up dying, all we are told is, "Sorry for your loss; we tried." I'm sure the medical staff must feel like hell, having to tell family members their loved one has died.

Is the money going where they say it is—for research—or is it being taken up by the organization coordinators and administrators to use as they see fit, whatever that might be? Maybe they should be held more accountable to the public. I have heard that very little of the donated money actually gets to the cause. True or not, it makes me less inclined to give.

Sometimes the doctors must feel like theirs is a thankless job. We need to say thank you to them; they never seem to give up. Then we hear that if we donate more money, there soon will be a cure. Well, I'm done listening to that. I gave money for years, and still I'm losing people who should not be dying early in their lives, not to mention the agony they and their families experience during the tragic ordeal. Sometimes seeing your loved one die makes you feel guilty about not donating enough toward research for a possible cure.

It's too hard to even watch. It makes everyone involved sick at heart. It seems to be happening way too often these days. Is it our lifestyles and eating habits, or what could the answer be? Every time I turn around, somebody else I know has cancer. I don't remember it being so prevalent in the past.

Doctors say if you have any suspicion of cancer, see a doctor right away; treat it as serious and get it looked after. At least three of my relatives did that, but the doctor treated for other ailments before looking for cancer, and they were all stage four by the time they were diagnosed. They all succumbed in the end—such a needless waste. I wonder if deaths from dread diseases stem from cutbacks. I think it's possible.

Doctors can only do so much, and they have to search for underlying causes of ill health. Hopefully, one day soon, a blood test or something just as simple will be the solution for these dread diseases. Imagine if we were not aware that there are blood tests or other simple tests that work?

My father, at age forty-nine, had a few heart attacks; the doctor said it was his nerves. After about a year, Dad finally convinced the doctor to send him to a heart specialist. He had a massive heart attack the day before the appointment and died. The autopsy showed evidence of five previous heart attacks. Why did my dad have to try to convince the doctor it was not his nerves for an entire year before the doctor decided to help him? My dad was not a hypochondriac or even a sickly person. I only remember him being sick once ever in his life; then this. All these years later, we are still wondering and asking ourselves what else we should have done to convince the doctor earlier. Of course, that was not due to cutbacks. I think it was lack of knowledge at that time.

That was traumatic for the entire family. When the siblings get together for family functions, we still mention it once in a while. It is something we cannot understand. It has been a long time since Dad's passing, but my mother never recovered from it until the day she died, twelve years later. The doctor probably never knew what happened to my dad. I like to think my father helped the heart and stroke research somehow. I have had a couple of heart attacks and a stroke, and I know that advancements in heart and stroke research is what saved my life. I will be forever grateful to my medical staff. Because of them, I am here to sound off.

Great strides have been made in heart disease and strokes but not so much in cancer.

Chapter 24

RECOGNIZE A PROBLEM
BEFORE IT'S TOO LATE

Are there different standards for the well-off and the low-income families? The elite do not have the same problems that low-income families have. There's no immediate concern for the matter at hand. We are asking for recognition to help us with fundamentals, like food and housing, utilities, employment, day care, gas, debt. Get people back on their feet. Is the country in such bad shape that we need to go without necessities?

I believe politicians know what is needed. Isn't it possible to make it happen? Now that we have millions of people living below the poverty line, who is going to help us? I don't hear of anyone stepping up to the plate. Maybe it's time to donate a few million dollars to our own country's cause before sending it away generously to other countries. After all, it is our money. I understand that help is needed elsewhere, but we need help at the moment as well. Canada is known as very generous to other countries' causes, and that is something of which we should be proud. Hopefully, we will be in a better position to do it again, but right now we need to concentrate on us—our children and elderly, and those who are ill, homeless, less fortunate, hungry, disabled, and needy. We also need to focus on home health care, nursing homes and day care centers. We need these things, but we also need safe havens for those in need.

It seems very unfair that sports players in this country make more money than, say, those who serve in the armed forces, who put their lives on the line for long periods of time. Doctors, who spend years of their lives in school so they can save our lives; police officers; fire fighters; nurses; and other professionals who care are not shown a lot of respect for their efforts. These are the dedicated members of society who deserve the best we can give of our support and in financial compensation. It seems to be all about how much money you make. How can the sports world be justified in their high salaries, yet the professionals we actually need for survival have limits set on their earnings? It's unfair and unbalanced that a country such as ours would value entertainment over their citizens' lives? *That* is the bottom line.

Of course, people in a lower wage bracket cannot afford the luxury of attending sports games with their families. Maybe the team could do a game once in a while for their not-so-rich hometown fans at a discount price. They could show the little ones how it is to be a famous sports figure. Even a charity event where the price of a ticket would be a donation could be a wonderful gesture. That would probably be the thrill of their young lives.

Chapter 25

FINANCIAL ISSUES

Some issues so big in our everyday lives that I wonder if we will even survive this era of a seemingly unmotivated and uncaring government. The decision is whether to feed our children or pay the outrageous monthly household debt, like heat, electricity, food, or taxes. Of course we feed our children first, but therein lies the problem. We need to look after our families, and that takes money that many people do not have. Clothing for youngsters also is a necessity. Some family members check with parents of children to make sure they have seasonal outer garments. It almost takes grandparents, aunts, uncles, and other relatives to help young parents make homes for their families.

In some areas, power was cut off for many residents for months. The usage fee was not that high; mostly it's the other fees added on that make it impossible to pay. Wages, electricity, heat, food, housing, and day care need urgent attention, along with health care.

Our government representatives don't relate to these particular problems. They do not live this way, so they don't see it in their everyday world. It seems there is another world out there where we citizens of moderate and low incomes do not belong. It is absolutely mind-boggling from our viewpoint that money is not an issue for the elite, who do not want to admit that there are serious problems very near to them. Do they expect the issues to just melt away? Well, that is not happening, and it is getting critical for a lot of people. Try to imagine how hopeless these people feel. How can we ease their worried minds. How can we benefit all areas that need attention?

Now a new carbon tax has been added. When is it going to end? I truly am concerned and worried. Let's see if change can take place in our lifetimes.

Chapter 26

FAIR PLAY

The sense of fair play has been destroyed by large conglomerates that seem to have monopolized the world of communications and that charge outrageous fees for every service they offer. They don't seem to care one iota about consumers, as long as their greed is satisfied. Anytime I've dealt with them in the past (one of them in particular), they were rude to me. After speaking with others, it is still going on today.

Is there no regulating body over these companies? They offer numerous TV channels, but after we sign a contract to receive a few hundred, we find out the same shows are on eight channels at the same time. Isn't that misrepresentation? Can't someone do something about it? Why can't we purchase only the channels we actually want? There should be a ceiling on their profits or at least a limit on charges to the public. Communication companies are so few that there seem to be limited choices, and they dictate how it is going to be. Why are they allowed to hold a monopoly on the business? (It seems like they do.)

Another complaint many have are the Cell phone companies' outrageous charges. Why do the charges have to be so high? When we purchase electronics, we barely get them home before they are outdated. Why not guarantee them for, say, five years at least? Maybe this would help the consumers.

I would like to see a phone that is only a phone for emergencies, with no apps or magical anything on it. That sounds good to me. These companies are so inventive; why don't they come up with devices that will last longer. They must have that capability.

Chapter 27

SOME THINGS WE CAN'T CHANGE, BUT WE WON'T KNOW UNTIL WE TRY

There is a mounting crisis for our seniors, with regard to trouble and standards in nursing homes, as well as the cost. More seniors are opting to stay in their homes, but that requires outside help that not everyone can acquire. It seems simple, but it is not that easy.

Family members usually have to help the nursing home staff come up with a program and schedule that works for the individual. Some of the programs don't meet specific requirements of the aging. Care for different illnesses and disabilities are not always met, so the senior is left without a service that he or she requires.

My stroke left me with a weak right side, and I managed to exercise back to reasonable movement, except for my right ankle, which seems permanently frozen to some extent and makes walking awkward for me. I have had several PSWs try to help, even though they are not trained in therapy. Just massaging the ankle feels good, and a few visits to therapy clinics helped for a while too. They try but are allowed to do only seven treatments a year under health care payments. Each time I get to the same point, and I'm told to come back next year. That will give me the same treatments over seven visits as the one I just completed. It makes no sense; it just does not go far enough to correct the problem. The health plan no longer covers this therapy, and therapy is needed by thousands of patients for healing. It seems to cover maybe a half or a third of the recovery that one might require.

That seems like building half a barn and waiting for the other half to build itself. It just doesn't work that way. A one-time complete treatment process that works would be better than seven or so without results, doing the same things over and over and costing the health plan more in time. I guess they have a routine program set by professionals, who know the ins and outs of the business and a budget to which they must adhere. Some people will never get beyond a certain point, and that is often not helpful.

Other people have chronic issues that probably need continuing therapy. Life expectancy is longer now but a long life is not special if it is painful and causes irritation. A little comfort goes a long way for these kinds of ailments.

I have called a few private occupational and massage therapists. The least expensive was eighty dollars an hour, and lots of them are around the hundred-dollar range. I cannot afford that, so I have to live with my discomfort.

Chapter 28

THOSE WHO ARE ABLE SHOULD HELP

I am appealing to the government on behalf of all people, average-to low-income Canadians, to work with us to make a safer world for our children and young people so they may grow up confident in our country and become contributing members of society with confidence and dignity.

I hear our contribution to the clean-air solution will be substantial. Kudos for that.

I see television ads that feature our children asking for help with environmental issues. If citizens and government worked together, who knows what we would accomplish? I think it's worth the effort. We have to start somewhere soon to make it work.

Who would have thought the idea would be presented by our beloved children? When I think of our young people today, I realize no other generation has had so many instruments to help them learn. Today's children are the most intelligent generation and are going to use their knowledge wisely with the tools provided to them by their elders.

We are putting our faith in you, young folks. May love and prosperity be in your lives always.

We also would like Canada to remain a world leader and a beautiful country, with all our nationalities working together within our different cultures but having the same dreams. There *is* harmony here.

With our neighbor to the south having a new president in 2016 and with so many changes taking place there, Canada looks more inviting, and finally some respect is being paid to us. I think we have looked like the next-door neighbor for so long that it's time we got some recognition for our charm, intelligence, and integrity from other countries. We seem to have a reputation as a friendly, laid-back place, but it takes a lot of work by a lot of people to make it appear to run that smoothly. We have a lot to be proud of. Let's not forget to help your constituents who may have fallen on hard times. They deserve the time and effort from those who can make a difference. The situation is critical now, and I hate to think what will happen if we don't help them.

Let's put our differences aside and concentrate on the important issues. After all, our differences won't matter if we don't work together to survive. If we can do this, perhaps it will inspire better relations with others in similar circumstances to pull together. Maybe a fresh look and working problems out together is needed. We seem to be far apart on some issues, and they need to be discussed with groups of us who are concerned and can alleviate some of the divisiveness that exists now. It should make us feel more included in our decisions and political endeavors.

Some take note of one area that needs fixing, and others see different things that do. When we put a few together, it doesn't take long to figure out that we need to start somewhere soon. Brainstorming may be the answer.

You may remember a more peaceful time, growing up in Canada. It was nice to stroll through downtown Toronto at any time. My family and friends would do that frequently on the weekends and have a lovely day. Now it is not relaxing at all. There are areas where we don't even want to venture, where crime is common. It also seems as though there are more violent crimes every year; at least that is what the statistics show. Maybe it's because we crowd too many people into a small area. Everywhere you look there are skyscrapers. An aerial view of the city and suburbs must look like an ant colony. I live in the country now, and I love it here. There's a relaxing pace and very soothing to the nerves.

Chapter 29

IF ALL ELSE FAILS, TRY, TRY AGAIN

The crime world is the worst. Anyone who watches true crime stories or the news has seen the police use cameras to follow criminals and investigate by looking at surveillance tapes from the street, stores, parking lots, and anywhere we happen to walk or drive. They seem to get enough information to piece together someone's whereabouts at certain times of the day. It is necessary to help the authorities solve crimes, but it also takes away our privacy. I realize the idea is to keep us safe, and in the long run we do benefit from it. The question, however, is, what is happening to our beautiful city that we have to lose our freedom to thugs, drug dealers, and crime at such a horrendous rate?

Perhaps it's because we just don't have enough money for the manpower to correct the problem. This is a good example of charity beginning at home. Let's take care of our own serious situation before worrying about impressing other countries.

This is our country. Let's look after home first. Then we can send help elsewhere, after we get on our feet. Our representatives should make us feel like we are worth their efforts, and they should keep their election promises. It seems to me that they don't care at all otherwise.

We need help, and we need it now. Do they think we don't need help? We sure do.

Please help us to pay our debts, buy or rent a home, get the necessary supplies to run a home, and look after our children properly. Please take another look at the cost of electricity, health care, and pharmaceuticals. Right now, certain people are taking unfair advantage of us, and we simply can't afford for them to do that. They seem to make their own rules and get away with it by running things the way they want.

Take a look at how supermarkets think up new ways to trick us into thinking we are getting a great deal, but it isn't so. The stores are out to make a profit at our expense. Someone must think we are gullible. We certainly are not. We have no way to help ourselves without also breaking laws. We shouldn't have to ask for or demand proper treatment and honesty from these businesses. They should build their reputations on fairness and integrity. Why are they not penalized so they don't do it again? Why aren't they made to follow the law? A simple fine or slap on the wrist is not enough for them. They go right back at it.

Do you agree that it is way past time to correct these situations, make changes to these adult bullies, and have them answer to authorities who can deal with them legally? We simply cannot let them have the upper hand any longer. We need help with this and want to start living in peace once again.

It will be wonderful when we all can prosper, to some degree, by the rules. Getting along and helping one another wouldn't be a bad new beginning.

One thing is for sure: I don't want to die knowing that our precious children will inherit this mess from us. We need to clear up what we can and leave clean water and air so they will have a good start at making changes. I think they will be more than capable of that in their lifetimes. I believe we owe them that much.

It would be wonderful if the young ones did not have these

worries hanging over them as they start out as adults. Does anyone think they are worth the time and effort to try? The more we can settle and take care of now, the better off they will be. What a wonderful thought.